Mother's Day!

The Child's World®
childsworld.com

Published by The Child's World®
1980 Lookout Drive • Mankato, MN 56003-1705
800-599-READ • www.childsworld.com

Photographs ©: Kirin Photo/iStockphoto, cover,
1; Mediaphotos/iStockphoto, 5; Monkey Business
Images/Shutterstock Images, 6, 20; Agnieszka
Kirinicjanow/iStockphoto, 8–9; Shutterstock Images,
10, 16; Tomsickova Tatyana/Shutterstock Images, 13;
PeopleImages/iStockphoto, 15; iStockphoto, 18–19

Design Element: Shutterstock Images

ISBN 9781503816534
LCCN 2016945630

Printed in the United States of America
PA02324

ABOUT THE AUTHOR
M. J. York is a writer and editor
from Minnesota. She enjoys spring
rains and planting her garden.

Contents

Mother's Day

It is Mother's Day! I love my Mom!

6

We celebrate Mother's Day in May. We show Mom how much we care.

Special Gifts

We pick out a special card for Mom. I make one myself.

We get Mom a gift. We make art for her, too!

I pick out flowers for Mom.

We put them in a **vase**.

A Special Day

We let Mom sleep late.
We bring her breakfast
in bed.

Happy Mother's Day!

We spend the day with Mom. We have a **picnic** in the park.

We help Mom.

We do **chores**.

19

We **visit** grandmothers and aunts. Do you celebrate Mother's Day?

Picture Frame Craft

Make your mom a picture frame for Mother's Day!

Supplies:

8 craft sticks
glue
scissors

a photo or drawing
markers or other
    decorations

Instructions:

1. Set down two craft sticks to make the left and right sides of a square. Glue the other two on top to make the top and bottom of the square.

2. Cut your photo or drawing to fit in the square. Glue it on the square.

3. Make another square with the other four sticks. Glue it on top of the photo.

4. Decorate the square with markers or anything you like.

Glossary

chores — (CHORS) Chores are jobs you have to do often. We do chores around the house.

picnic — (PIK-nik) A picnic is a trip to eat a meal outdoors. We had a picnic in the park.

vase — (VAYS) A vase is a container for flowers. We put flowers and water in a vase.

visit — (VIZ-it) To visit is to go see other places or people. We visit our family.

To Learn More

Books

Miller, Reagan. *Mother's Day and Other Family Days*. New York, NY: Crabtree Publishing, 2011.

Trueit, Trudi Strain. *Mother's Day Crafts*. Mankato, MN: The Child's World, 2017.

Web Sites

Visit our Web site for links about Mother's Day: **childsworld.com/links**

Note to Parents, Teachers, and Librarians: We routinely verify our Web links to make sure they are safe and active sites. So encourage your readers to check them out!

Index